CODE READER™

Making Difficult Words Easy

Code Reader Books provide codes with "sound keys" to help read difficult words. For example, a word that may be difficult to read is "unicorn," so it might be followed by a code like this: unicorn (YOO-nih-korn). By providing codes with phonetic sound keys, Code Reader Books make reading easier and more enjoyable.

Examples of Code Reader™ Keys

Long a sound (as in make):
a *(with a silent e)* or **ay**
Examples: able *(AY-bul)*; break *(brake)*

Short i sound (as in sit): **i** or **ih**
Examples: myth *(mith)*; mission *(MIH-shun)*

Long i sound (as in by):
i *(with a silent e)* or **y**
Examples: might *(mite)*; bicycle *(BY-sih-kul)*

Keys for the long o sound (as in hope):
o *(with a silent e)* or **oh**
Examples: molten *(MOLE-ten)*; ocean *(OH-shen)*

Codes use dashes between syllables *(SIH-luh-buls)*, and stressed syllables have capital letters.

To see more Code Reader sound keys, see page 44.

ICE AGE
CREATURES
(KREE-CHURZ)

Ice Age Creatures

A Code Reader™ Book
Green Series

_____

Reading Consultant: Jennifer L. VanSlander, Ph.D., Asst. Professor of Educational Leadership, Columbus State University

Code Readers™ is a trademark of Treasure Bay, Inc.

Patent Pending.
Code Reader books are designed using an innovative system of methods to create and include phonetic codes to enhance the readability of text. Reserved rights include any patent rights.

Published by
Treasure Bay, Inc.
PO Box 519
Roseville, CA 95661 USA

Printed in China

Library of Congress Control Number: 2024944968

ISBN: 978-1-60115-725-6

Visit us online at: CodeReader.org

PR-1-25

CONTENTS

An "ice age" is a long period *(PEER-ree-ud)* of time on Earth when temperatures *(TEM-pur-uh-churz)* fall around the world. The last ice age ended about 10,000 years ago, and this is what is generally referred to as the Ice Age.

During this period, vast grasslands developed along with large areas of ice and snow. The grasses and shrubs allowed a great variety *(vuh-RY-eh-tee)* of creatures *(KREE-churz)* to thrive. Both plant-eaters and meat-eaters were able to find plenty of food.

Plant-eaters, such as mammoth, sloths, and bison *(BY-sun)*, grew large. Big predators, such as saber-toothed *(SAY-bur-tooth-t)* cats, dire wolves *(wulvs)*, and cave bears, fed on the giant *(JY-ent)* plant-eaters and also grew large. Even birds were giant during the Ice Age!

After an animal dies, it may get covered by water and dirt. If conditions are right, fossils will form from the animal's bones. Scientists *(SY-en-tists)* study these fossils to learn about extinct *(ex-TINKT)* animals.

In 2012, foot bones of a dire wolf *(wulf)* were discovered near Tule *(TOO-lee)* Springs Fossil Beds in Nevada *(neh-VAD-uh)*. There are many fossils in this area, but this was the first dire wolf fossil to be found there.

Some dead animals may become mummified (*MUM-ih-fide*). Many Ice Age animals have been found mummified in permafrost, a thick layer of soil just below the surface (*SUR-fus*) that remains frozen for many years. These mummified animals give scientists lots of information (*in-for-MAY-shun*) as the animal's flesh, skin, and fur may be preserved (*pree-ZURVD*). The remains can be thousands of years old, but they may look like the animal just died.

5

California's La Brea *(BRAY-uh)* Tar Pits trapped thousands of animals during the Ice Age. The animals waded into the pool of liquid *(LIK-wid)* asphalt *(AS-fawlt)*—a thick, black oil and tar-like substance that bubbled up from underground. Like quicksand, the sticky asphalt made it impossible for the animals to escape, trapping them in the tar until they died.

When large plant-eaters, like mammoths and wild horses, got stuck in the asphalt, meat-eaters would enter to grab them. Then they became stuck, too!

The fossils that scientists have found in the tar pits have helped them to learn *(lurn)* about many of the animals that lived during the Ice Age.

Ice age mammoths were mammals. Similar to modern elephants, they had a long trunk that hung from their flat faces which they used to smell things and pick up food. They had two very large tusks on either side of their trunk. Some mammoth tusks grew up to 15 feet long.

The mammoths we usually *(YOO-zhoo-uh-lee)* think of today are woolly mammoths. They lived from about 120,000 to 3,700 years ago—during the Ice Age and well past it! Their shaggy hair ranged in color from blonde *(blond)* to black. Under their skin, woolly mammoths had a four-inch layer of fat to help keep them warm.

MAMMOTHS AROUND THE WORLD

= woolly mammoth range

NORTH AMERICA

COSTA RICA
(KOS-tuh REE-kuh)

WOOLLY MAMMOTHS

They lived throughout *(throo-OWT)* Europe *(YUR-rup)*, northern Asia *(AY-zhuh)*, and parts of North America.

COLUMBIAN *(Kuh-LUM-bee-an)* MAMMOTHS

They lived throughout much of North America from Canada *(KAN-uh-duh)* to Costa Rica.

EUROPE

ASIA

Long ago, people living on the island of Crete *(kreet)*
found huge skeletons. The skulls had large teeth and
long tusks. Each skull had a big hole in the middle.
It looked like an eye socket. People put the bones
together to make something that looked like a giant,
with one eye and huge fangs! But the bones had been
put together the wrong way. The remains were actually
(AK-choo-uh-lee) from an ancient *(AYN-chent)* mammoth
relative *(REL-luh-tiv)*.

Mammoths and humans *(HYOO-munz)* lived at the same time and scientists have learned that humans hunted them. Experts once believed *(beh-LEEVD)* they hunted the large animals by chasing them off cliffs. Then, in 2018, scientists examined *(eg-ZAM-und)* a fossilized mammoth rib and found a piece of flint spearhead *(SPEER-hed)* stuck in it. The spearhead could have come from only one source: human hunters!

Thousands of years ago, early humans created *(kree-AY-ted)* art on the walls of caves. They would carve or paint on the rock walls. The artwork told stories, mainly about hunting. Many different animals were depicted *(deh-PIK-tid)*. A cave in France is called the Cave of the Hundred Mammoths. Most of the animals pictured on these cave walls are mammoths.

Mammoth Graveyard

In 1974, a man named George *(jorj)* Hanson was leveling ground in Hot Springs, South Dakota *(dah-KOH-tah)*. One day, his shovel *(SHUV-el)* hit something in the dirt. It was a 7-foot-long mammoth tusk! Hanson soon found other fossils. A team of professors and students came to the site to help excavate *(EX-kuh-vate)*, or dig up, the fossils. Today, this area is known as the Mammoth Site of Hot Springs, South Dakota.

MAMMOTH SOCIETY (suh-SY-ih-tee) FACT

Adult mammoths took huge steps while walking. The calves *(cavz)* had to run to keep up with the adults!

The last mammoths are thought *(thawt)* to have lived on an island *(I-land)* in the Arctic *(ARK-tik)* Ocean *(OH-shun)*. Rising ocean levels cut this area off from the mainland. New mammoths could not get there. Generations *(jen-ur-AY-shuns)* of mating with relatives caused the woolly mammoths to lose their sense of smell and their hair became silky instead of woolly and warm. The small population *(pop-yoo-LAY-shun)* could not recover. They died around 4,000 years ago.

Dire wolves were fierce *(FEERes)* predators that lived during the Ice Age. Their scientific name, *Canis dirus (DEE-roos)*, means "fearsome dog." They are an extinct relative of modern gray wolves and are part of the family of animals that includes wolves, coyotes *(KY-oh-tees)*, foxes, and dogs.

Dire wolves lived in many different places. They roamed mountain forests and dry grasslands.

DIRE WOLVES

They lived throughout North and South America.

NORTH AMERICA

SOUTH AMERICA

DIRE WOLVES

Dire wolves looked similar to other canids *(CAN-idz)*. They had thick fur. Their fur varied in color from black and gray to rusty brown. Their broad heads had upright ears.

DIRE WOLF

GRAY WOLF

Dire wolves had short, powerful legs. They were more than five feet long from the tip of their pointed nose to the end of their bushy tail and weighed *(wade)* 125 to 175 pounds. Dire wolves were about 25 percent larger than gray wolves.

Gray wolves and dire wolves lived in the same areas, but they did not compete for food. Gray wolves hunted deer and other fast prey *(pray)*. Dire wolves took down slower moving animals, such as ancient *(AYN-chent)* bison.

While gray wolves are still living today, dire wolves became extinct about 10,000 years ago.

Studying modern red and gray wolves helped scientists learn how dire wolves lived long ago. Like other wolves, they were social *(SOH-shul)* animals that lived in family groups *(groops)* called packs. The pack was led by two wolves—the alpha *(AL-fuh)* male and the alpha female *(FEE-male)*. "Alpha" means they were the top-ranking animals in the pack. They were the first to eat after a kill and many experts believe that only the alpha pair had pups.

Dire wolves dug underground holes, called dens. The alpha female gave birth to her pups in the den. There were probably *(PRAH-bub-lee)* between one and nine pups, the same number that gray wolves have. The adults would often leave to go hunting, but the pups stayed safe inside their den.

The pups grew quickly. At first, they drank milk from their mother. After several weeks, they got their first taste of meat. Their mother would eat the meat first, then regurgitate *(ree-GUR-jih-tate)*, or throw up, the chewed meat for the pups. This may sound nasty, but this meal was delicious *(dee-LISH-us)* to the dire wolf pups!

After a few months, the pups were able to leave the den and travel with the rest of the pack. At first, they just followed *(FAH-lode)*, watching and learning *(LUR-ning)*. But by the time they were a year old, they were actively hunting with the rest of the pack.

Dire wolves were hypercarnivores *(HY-pur-KAR-nih-vors)*. That means that more than 70 percent of their diet was meat. The rest came from plants and berries. Research *(REE-surch)* suggests *(suh-JESTS)* that humans and dire wolves hunted the same kinds of animals. This competition *(kom-peh-TIH-shun)* for food may be part of the reason dire wolves died out.

DIRE WOLF SOCIETY FACT

Dire wolves seemed to enjoy eating Ice Age horses. Their remains have been found together at many fossil sites.

In a few cases, scientists have found the remains of dire wolves that had been hurt or wounded *(WOON-ded)*. It looked like their wounds had healed before the wolves died. This led scientists to believe that these wolves cared for injured *(IN-jurd)* pack members. This behavior *(bee-HAYV-yur)* would have been something only dire wolves did. Other kinds of wolves leave injured members behind.

As top predators, dire wolves relied on a steady population of slow-moving prey. At the end of the Ice Age, many large plant eaters became extinct. Unlike gray wolves, dire wolves were not fast enough to catch deer and other fast-moving prey. Researchers believe this may be one reason dire wolves died out.

During the Ice Age, giant birds thundered across the land and soared overhead. Monster birds ruled both on the land and in the sky.

Teratorns *(TAIR-uh-torns)*, a kind of bird similar to modern vultures *(VUL-churs)* and eagles *(EE-guls)*, flew through the air. Experts believe these teratorns looked a lot like modern condors.

California *(kal-ih-FORN-yuh)* and Andean *(AN-dee-un)* condors are among the biggest flying birds alive today. Until recently few California condors remained in the wild. Researchers caught *(kawt)* the birds and bred them in captivity, then released them. Today, there are about 500 of these rare birds in the wild.

Andean condors are also rare in the wild. But they are easy to spot when they are flying. Each has about a 10-foot wingspan!

At nearly 10 feet tall, the *Kelenken* may have been the tallest, fastest terror bird. It had the largest skull and strongest bite.

Ice Age birds known as "terror birds" were different than the teratorns. Like the modern ostrich, they could not fly. They had small wings, but they hunted on the ground and ran quickly to catch prey.

The small but fierce *(FEERes)* *Psilopterus* *(sy-LOP-teh-rus)* were terror birds who stood just over two feet tall. They were relatively *(rel-uh-TIV-lee)* heavy for their size, weighing *(WAY-ing)* about 15 pounds. Scientists think that this bird leaped onto unsuspecting prey then used its sharp claws to tear *(tare)* the prey apart. Fossils of this bird suggest it may have lived as recently as 6,300 years ago.

TITANIS (TY-tan-eez) TERROR BIRD ATTACKING A HAGERMAN HORSE

Some large, aggressive terror birds would chase down their prey then violently *(VY-oh-lent-lee)* shake the prey in the air before smashing it to pieces on the ground.

An Ice Age teratorn called called *Aiolornis* (AY-oh-LUR-nee) *incredibilis* (in-KRED-ih-BIL-lis) was first discovered in Nevada in 1952. Out of nearly 650 bird bones, only a single bone from its wing was found. But it was enough (ee-NUF) for scientists to recognize a new species of monster bird. Later fossil finds led scientists to agree that this bird had a massive beak capable (KAPE-uh-bul) of shredding prey.

South America's *Brontornis* (brawn-TOR-nis) stood more than nine feet tall. It is also called the thunder bird.

Bird bones have air holes inside them. This makes them lightweight (*LITE-wayt*) and helps birds fly. But these bones are fragile (*FRA-jul*) and do not preserve well.

Scientists are not sure why monster birds died out. They suspect the changing climate *(KLY-met)* caused aggressive predators, such as saber-toothed cats and dire wolves, to spread into their territory *(TARE-rih-tor-ee)*. They hunted the giant birds who could not protect themselves against these powerful predators. It is possible that loss of habitat was also a contributing *(kun-TRIB-yoo-ting)* factor in their path to extinction *(ex-TINK-shun)*.

Some of the most well-known and popular *(POP-yoo-lur)* of the Ice Age animals are the saber-toothed cats. Strong and fierce, their fangs were like long sabers or curved swords.

Members of the cat family, they are distantly related to lions, cheetahs, tigers, and domestic cats. These large cats lived all over the world but are now extinct.

31

More than a dozen *(DUZ-en)* different species *(SPEE-sheez)* of saber-toothed cats roamed the Earth during the Ice Age. They lived all over the world except in the Arctic and Antarctica *(ant-ARK-tih-kah)*.

One type of saber-tooth cat is the *Smilodon (SMY-luh-don)*. These Ice Age cats are often called saber-toothed *tigers*, although *(awl-THOH)* they are not tigers at all. These cats were about seven feet long from head to tail. They stood four feet tall at the shoulder and weighed up to 800 pounds. That's about twice as heavy as a modern lion. Their tails were short and stubby bobtails, but their front canine *(KAY-nine)* teeth were long—up to eight inches long!

Homotherium *(HOH-muh-THEE-ree-um)* were another kind of saber-toothed cat. Its fangs were only about 4 inches long, but it had long legs that probably helped it run fast when chasing prey.

At one time, scientists believed these saber-toothed cats died out in Europe around 300,000 years ago. But in the year 2000, a fishing boat in the North Sea hauled *(hawld)* up a strange jawbone. Tests revealed the jawbone was from *Homotherium* *(HOH-muh-THEE-ree-um)* and was just 28,000 years old. Experts were shocked! Now we know these cats lived more recently than previously *(PREE-vee-us-lee)* thought!

The oldest saber-toothed cat fossils are from *Megantereon* *(meg-en-TARE-ee-un)*. They were found in North America and are over 4.5 million years old. A full skeleton of this cat was once found in France.

These cats were about the size of a modern jaguar *(JAG-wahr)* and they weighed as much as 330 pounds. Scientists believe they behaved like leopards *(LEP-urdz)*. After killing large prey, they dragged it into a tree to keep it away from other animals.

Ancient bison *(BY-sun)*, mammoths, and giant sloths roamed the abundant grasslands during the Ice Age. Food was plentiful for these plant-eaters. But their presence *(PREZ-ens)* attracted the attention *(uh-TEN-shun)* of many large carnivores, including the saber-toothed cats. The large plant-eaters were slow-movers and easy prey for the big cats.

Most saber-toothed cats did not chase their prey. Instead, they hunted by hiding and then leaping on their prey in a surprise attack.

Some remains of these cats have been found with broken bones. They were likely injured by powerful blows from mammoth tusks when they attempted to take down a small, young member of a mammoth herd.

Xenosmilus (ZEE-noh-SMY-lus) were yet another type of saber-toothed cat. Two skeletons of this cat were found in the United (yoo-NY-ted) States, in Florida. Also at the site were a large number of bones of a pig-like animal called a peccary (PEK-uh-ree). These cats had short legs and widely spaced teeth, which made researchers think they hunted differently from their relatives. Nicknamed "cookie cutter cats," they probably bit chunks of flesh out the flanks of the peccary then waited for their prey to bleed to death before eating it.

Saber-toothed cats most likely lived their lives much the same way as modern African *(AF-rih-kan)* lions. It is believed that they lived in groups, called prides. And, like lions, they may have cared for sick or injured members of their group.

SABER-TOOTHED CAT SOCIETY *(suh-SY-ih-tee)* **FACT**

Scientists think saber-toothed cats lived in groups like the African lions do today. This photo shows a pride of modern lions.

Scientists are not sure why saber-toothed cats grew long canine *(KAY-nine)* teeth. These big cats may have used their long teeth to puncture *(PUNK-chur)* animals' throats or slice into their soft bellies. Or these huge teeth could have been just for show. Competing male cats may have scared off rivals *(RY-vulz)* by showing their dagger-like fangs. Female cats may have been more impressed by the males with the largest teeth.

As the Ice Age came to an end, large prey animals died out. Only small, swift prey remained. Early antelopes and horses were fast. Much like the dire wolves, the big saber-toothed cats could not catch them. The smaller, more fleet-footed cats were more successful *(suk-SES-ful)*. By the end of the Ice Age, saber-toothed cats were gone.

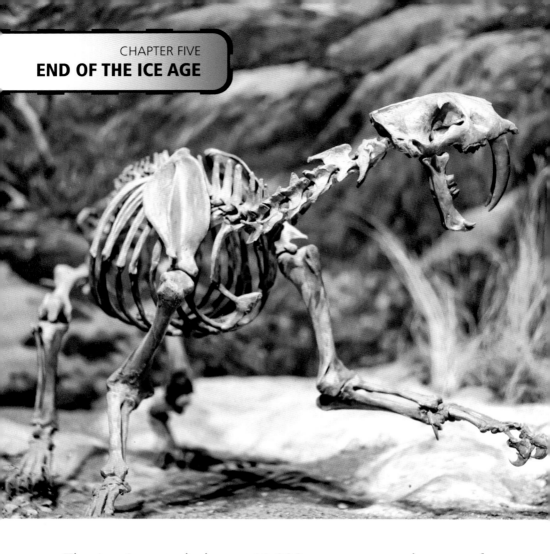

The Ice Age ended over 11,000 years ago and many of the animals from that time are now extinct. Lucky for us, scientists and researchers have unearthed *(un-URTHT)* fossils and mummified remains of these animals. From these remains, they have been able to create models of what these animals looked like. A visit to a museum *(myoo-ZEE-um)* of natural history lets you see some of these models and fossils up close.

If you are hoping to see more than a skeleton or model of these animals, you may not have long to wait. Scientists who study woolly mammoth remains have sometimes been able to take out parts of their DNA. DNA is what helps determine *(dee-TER-min)* the features *(FEE-churs)* of living things. One day, scientists may be able to replace some elephant DNA with woolly mammoth DNA, and an elephant may have a baby that looks like a woolly mammoth!

GLOSSARY

alpha *(AL-fuh)* **animal**: the top-ranking, and usually most powerful, animal in a particular social group

excavation *(EX-kuh-VAY-shun)*: the act of digging, especially when something specific, such as fossils or bones, are being removed from the ground

fossil *(FAH-sul)*: the remains or traces of plants and animals that lived a long time ago

hypercarnivore *(HY-per-KAR-nih-vor)*: an animal that has a diet that is more than 70 percent meat

La Brea *(luh BRAY-uh)* **Tar Pits**: marshes of bubbling quicksand-like tar, located in Los Angeles, California, containing fossils of prehistoric animals that were trapped in the muck

saber *(SAY-ber)*: a heavy sword with a curved blade

Smilodon *(SMY-luh-don)*: a type of saber-toothed cat from the Ice Age; though not related to modern tigers, it is often called a saber-toothed tiger

teratorn *(TAIR-uh-torn)*: an extinct group of giant flying birds of prey

QUESTIONS TO THINK ABOUT

1. What are some things that animals needed to thrive during the Ice Age?

2. How do you think pack animals like dire wolves work together to bring down prey? Can you think of any modern wild animals that also hunt this way?

3. The "terror birds" of the Ice Age did not fly. Do you know of any birds alive today that do not fly?

4. What are some of the reasons that many Ice Age animals died out?

5. There is a chance that woolly mammoths may someday be recreated through science. Do you think this is a good thing or a bad thing and why?

6. If you wanted more information about Ice Age creatures, how might you try to get that information?

CODE READER™

Making Difficult Words Easy

Code Reader Books provide codes with "sound keys" to help read difficult words. For example, a word that may be challenging to read is "chameleon," so it might be followed by a code like this: chameleon *(kuh-MEE-lee-un)*.

The codes use phonetic keys for each sound in the word. Knowing the keys can help make reading the codes easier.

Code Reader™ Keys

Long a sound (as in make):
a *(with a silent e)*, **ai**, or **ay**
Examples: break *(brake)*;
area *(AIR-ee-uh)*; able *(AY-bul)*

Short a sound (as in cat): **a**
Example: practice *(PRAK-tis)*

Long e sound (as in keep): **ee**
Example: complete *(kum-PLEET)*

Short e sound (as in set): **e** or **eh**
Examples: metric *(MEH-trik)*;
bread *(bred)*

Long i sound (as in by):
i *(with a silent e)* or **y**
Examples: might *(mite)*;
bicycle *(BY-sih-kul)*

Short i sound (as in sit): **i** or **ih**
Examples: myth *(mith)*;
condition *(kun-DIH-shun)*

Long u sound (as in cube): **yoo**
Example: unicorn *(YOO-nih-korn)*

Short u or schwa sound (as in cup):
u or **uh**
Examples: pension *(PEN-shun)*;
about *(uh-BOWT)*

Long o sound (as in hope):
o (with a silent e), **oh**,
or **o** at the end of a syllable
Examples: molten *(MOLE-ten)*;
ocean *(OH-shen)*; nobody *(NO-bah-dee)*

Short o sound (as in top): **o** or **ah**
Examples: posture *(POS-chur)*;
bother *(BAH-ther)*

Long oo sound (as in cool): **oo**
Example: school *(skool)*

Short oo sound (as in look): **o͝o**
Examples: wood *(wo͝od)*;
could *(ko͝od)*

oy sound (as in boy): **oy**
Example: boisterous *(BOY-stur-us)*

ow sound (as in cow): **ow**
Example: discount *(DIS-kownt)*

aw sound (as in paw): **aw**
Example: faucet *(FAW-sit)*

qu sound (as in quit): **kw**
Example: question *(KWES-chun)*

zh sound (as in garage): **zh**
Example: fission *(FIH-zhun)*